Using the Dictionary

Workbook 1

This workbook belongs to:

_____

Published by
Heron Books, Inc.
20950 SW Rock Creek Road
Sheridan, OR 97378

heronbooks.com

_____

Special thanks to all the teachers and students who
provided feedback instrumental to this edition.

_____

Table of Contents

Note to the Teacher

The overall purpose of Using the Dictionary Workbook I is to raise a student's affinity for dictionaries.

More specific purposes include helping the child

- gain familiarity with dictionary content
- begin learning alphabetical order
- start using guide words to find entry words.

By the end of this workbook a student should have a strong understanding of alphabetical order and be able to find dictionary entries fairly easily. And he will have achieved this ability in a fun and interesting way!

This workbook has been designed for students reading well at a third-grade level or above.

Part I of this workbook is designed to allow a student to make his or her own discoveries while gaining a familiarity with what kinds of things can be found in dictionaries. There should be no need for correction or a search for "right answers." In this part of the workbook, the "Teacher Check" is simply an acknowledgement that a student has done the page.

After Part I, students should be observed closely to ensure success as they proceed through the workbook. A "Teacher Check" is provided on most pages, but these can be used on an individual basis, depending upon the needs of the student. If appropriate, a target of several pages can be given, then checked. If the activities prove inadequate for a given student to achieve the above purposes, particularly alphabetizing skills, ensure the student is given extra assistance to achieve confidence before moving on.

Dictionaries Recommended for Use with This Workbook

A key to success is having a number of different dictionaries appropriate to the student's reading level. For these purposes, three levels of dictionary are described.

Level 1: Beginning dictionaries such as *The DK Illustrated Dictionary*, *The Oxford First Illustrated Dictionary*, *American Heritage First Dictionary*, or other simple picture dictionaries.

Level 2: Dictionaries such as *Oxford Junior Illustrated Dictionary* or the *Schoolhouse Dictionary* (now out of print but useful if you have one) or similar basic dictionary, recommended for most activities.

Level 3: *Oxford Illustrated Children's Dictionary*, the *Scholastic Children's Dictionary*, *Oxford Primary Dictionary*, or a similar dictionary, recommended for limited use and mostly for comparison purposes.

Students should primarily use dictionaries of their own choosing, but the above information can be used by a conscientious teacher to help ensure student success. Note particularly that the third group of dictionaries can appear simple while in fact the content of the entries, the symbols or the language used is often too complex for young students. Used with judgment as ability and understanding increases, however, they can be beneficial and enjoyed by the student.

Materials Needed (In Addition to Dictionaries)

- A set of alphabet tiles
- 3 dice or cubes with a letter on each side

Note to the Student

This workbook is to help you have some fun while learning a little bit more about the dictionary.

When doing the activities, it is a good idea to use many different dictionaries so you get an idea of how they are similar and how they are different.

If you have any questions or something does not seem to make sense, talk to your teacher right away.

Some activities in this workbook have a box next to each step where you can write a check mark or put a star when you finish the step. ☑

Have Fun!

There is so much to know about the world!

Every day brings the chance to learn something new!

The **dictionary** is a book full of words and their meanings. It can be a good friend who is there to help when you want to know something.

In this workbook, you will be looking inside some dictionaries to find out what's there.

Do These Steps

☐ Find where the dictionaries are kept in your classroom. How many different kinds are there? _____

☐ How many dictionaries in all? _____

☐ Does your teacher keep a dictionary near her desk? Have her show you the one she uses.

☐ Does your school have a library? If so, go there and find where the dictionaries are kept. Ask the librarian for help if you need it.

☐ In your school library, or in a class of older students, ask the librarian or teacher to show you the largest dictionary in your school.

Do This

- ☐ Find a dictionary. Draw and color the cover here • • • • • • • •

- ☐ Guess how many inches tall it is.

  | in. |

- ☐ Guess how many inches wide it is.

  | in. |

- ☐ Guess how many pages it has.

  | pages |

- ☐ Guess how many words might be in this dictionary.

  | words |

- ☐ Guess how many ounces it weighs.

  | oz. |

REMEMBER: oz. stands for "ounce". A paperclip weighs about 1 ounce.

Now Do This

Find a different dictionary. Repeat some of the guessing steps. Mark your answers on this chart. • • • •

	Your Guess
How tall?	
How wide?	
How many pages?	
How many words?	

Pictures Show What Things Are

As you know, dictionaries have pictures to show you what things look like.

This funny-looking camera is called an "Instant Camera". The photo comes out of the front after taking the picture.

Do This

Animals have different kinds of coverings to protect them. Choose a dictionary that has good pictures in it. Look at some of the animal pictures in it. Use tally marks ⦀⦀ to show how many of each kind of animal covering you notice. Try to find 5 of each kind.

feathers		
scales		
fur		
hard covering		
smooth skin		
other		

Do This

☐ Look inside a dictionary and find a picture of an animal you like.

☐ Now look in a different dictionary and see if it has a picture of that animal. Does this dictionary have one?   Yes ◯   No ◯

If the answer is "yes," is the picture exactly the same?   Yes ◯   No ◯

☐ Draw your animal in the space above.

☐ Show your drawing to another student.

When people travel, they go from one place to another. There are many ways people can travel. They can go on land, by water or in the air.

Do This

In a dictionary, find pictures of different things people can travel in. Put a check mark ✓ on this chart for each one you find.

	1	2	3	4	5	6	7	8	9	10
flies in the sky										
floats on water										
slides										
moves on 4 wheels										
moves on 2 wheels										
other										

If you could travel in anything - *real or imagined* - what would you like to travel in?

☐ Draw it here.

☐ Show your drawing to another student.

Sports are games people play where they use their bodies.

People have been playing sports for thousands of years. Some of the oldest sports are running and archery, where you use a bow to shoot arrows at a target.

Do This

Many dictionaries have pictures. But they don't all have pictures of the same things.

☐ Get a dictionary. Look at the pictures. When you find a picture of people playing a sport, write the name of the sport in column 1 below.

☐ Now get a different dictionary. Find pictures of sports in it. Write the names of the sports you find in column 2 below.

1	2
1.	
2.	
3.	
4.	
5.	

Do This

- ☐ What sport would you like to play?

  _____

- ☐ Find that sport in the dictionary and read what it says.

- ☐ Draw a picture of you playing that sport.

- ☐ Show your drawing to another student.

A **sandwich** is two or more slices of bread around a filling of cheese, meat, or some other food.

The word sandwich comes from a story about a rich man from England whose last name was Sandwich. Back in the 1700s he was playing a game of cards but did not want to stop to eat. He ordered a cook to put meat between pieces of bread so he could eat while he played and his fingers would not get the cards messy! Soon everyone was calling slices of bread with filling in between "a sandwich."

Did you know that Americans eat almost 300 MILLION sandwiches each day?

Let's Eat!

☐ Make a list of what you would put inside the best sandwich ever! • • • • •

☐ Draw your sandwich here.

☐ Look in a dictionary to find a picture of something you would like to eat for breakfast. Put a star in the box next to **dictionary 1** when you found it. Find a picture for each of the other meals listed.

☐ Now do the same steps using a different dictionary. Put the stars next to **dictionary 2**.

	breakfast	lunch	snack	dinner	dessert
dictionary 1					
dictionary 2					

☐ Which dictionary had pictures that you liked more?

_____

☐ Ask three students which food they like the most.

1. _____   2. _____   3. _____

A **musical instrument** is anything that can be used to make music.

For thousands of years and all over the world people have found things to make music with. One of the oldest musical instruments found was a **flute** made from a Mammoth tusk!

"Cool!"

The **bagpipe** is a musical instrument that people have been playing for a few thousand years!

☐ Find the word **bagpipe** in a dictionary. Read what it says.

☐ Have you ever heard someone play the **bagpipe** or the **flute**? If you want to hear what they sound like, ask your teacher to show you a short video so you can see and hear them.

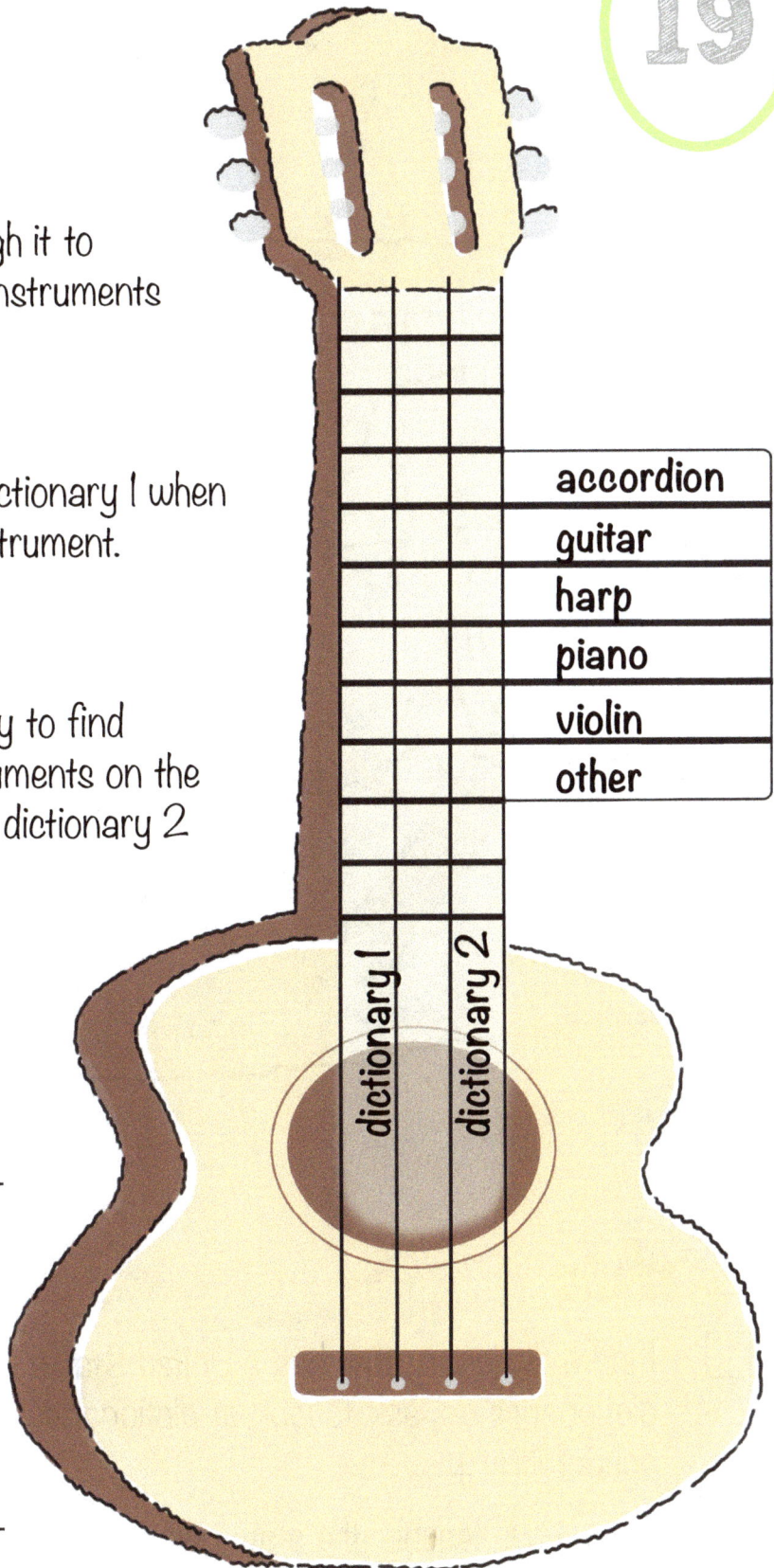

Do This

☐ Get a dictionary. Look through it to find pictures of the musical instruments on this list.

☐ Draw a star in the box for dictionary 1 when you find a picture of that instrument.

☐ Now get a different dictionary to find pictures of the musical instruments on the list. Put a star in the box for dictionary 2 when you find one.

☐ Which dictionary had pictures you liked more?

_____

☐ What instrument do you like the most?

_____

accordion
guitar
harp
piano
violin
other

dictionary 1
dictionary 2

A **map** is a drawing that shows where things are. A map can be of a town, a country or almost anything - even a building or a room!

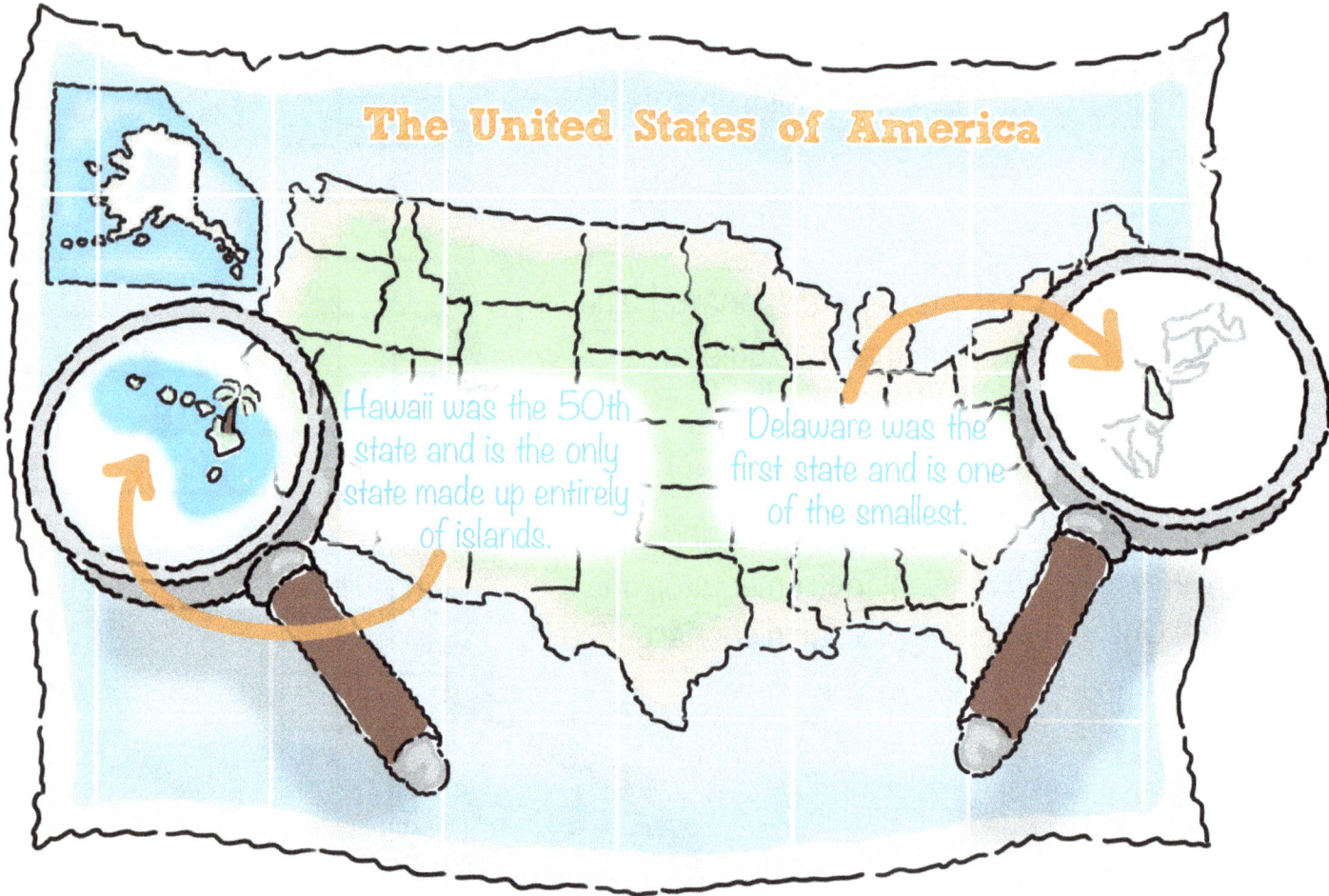

The United States of America

Hawaii was the 50th state and is the only state made up entirely of islands.

Delaware was the first state and is one of the smallest.

Some dictionaries have a map of the United States near the back of the book.

Do this

☐ Find a dictionary that has a United States map. If none of your classroom dictionaries do, ask to look at dictionaries from another classroom or your school library.

☐ Show your teacher the state you are in on the map.

☐ **Teacher Check**

Names of States

Some dictionaries have a list of the names of the 50 states. This list is usually found near the very end of the book.

☐ Find a dictionary that has a list of the names of the 50 States.

☐ Use it to do the steps below.

☐ What is the first state on the list?

_____

☐ What is the last state on the list?

_____

☐ Find the name of the state you are in right now.

_____

☐ Find the name of another state you have visited. If you have not yet been to another state, find the name of a state you would like to visit some day.

☐ Write the state here

_____

☐ Show another student the list of the 50 states. Have them tell you the name of a state they have visited or would like to visit. Find the name of that state on the list.

Write it here _____

22

The **world** is the Earth and all the oceans, land, plants, animals, and people on it.

In 1519 a man named Magellan was the first person to sail all the way around the world. The trip took 3 YEARS to complete!

In 1980, an airplane flew around the world in less than 3 days!

The Earth is 24,905 miles around.

There are 196 countries in the world.

Near the end of some dictionaries there is a list of all the countries on Earth. Some dictionaries also have a map of the world.

Let's Look

Look in some dictionaries, one at a time. Write "yes" or "no" to show if it has a list of countries or a map of the world.

	Has a list of countries	Has a map of the world
dictionary 1		
dictionary 2		
dictionary 3		
dictionary 4		

☐ Teacher Check

A **flag** is a piece of cloth with a special design on it that stands for a country or a group.

☐ Find a dictionary that has pictures of flags from the countries all around the world. You can look for these near the end of the dictionary.

☐ Look at the flags.

Choose the one you like.

Draw it here. Color it if you like.

Write the name of the country it stands for here.

_____

☐ Now draw a flag of your own here. Color it if you like.

☐ Show these flags to another student.

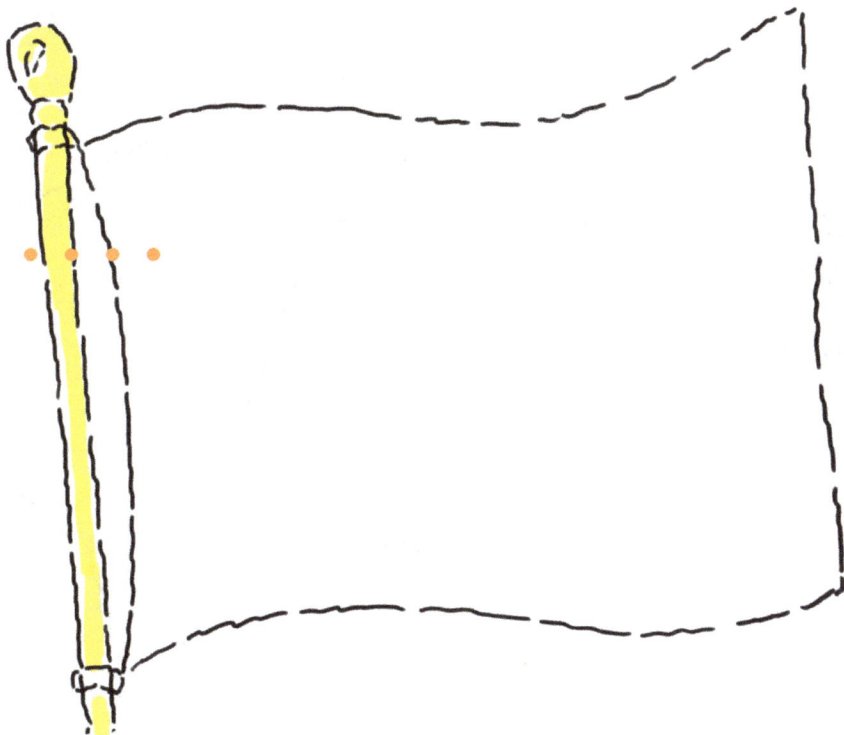

Dinosaurs were huge animals that lived on Earth over 65 million years ago.

The word dinosaur means "terrible lizard." One dinosaur, the Sauroposeidon grew over 50 feet tall!

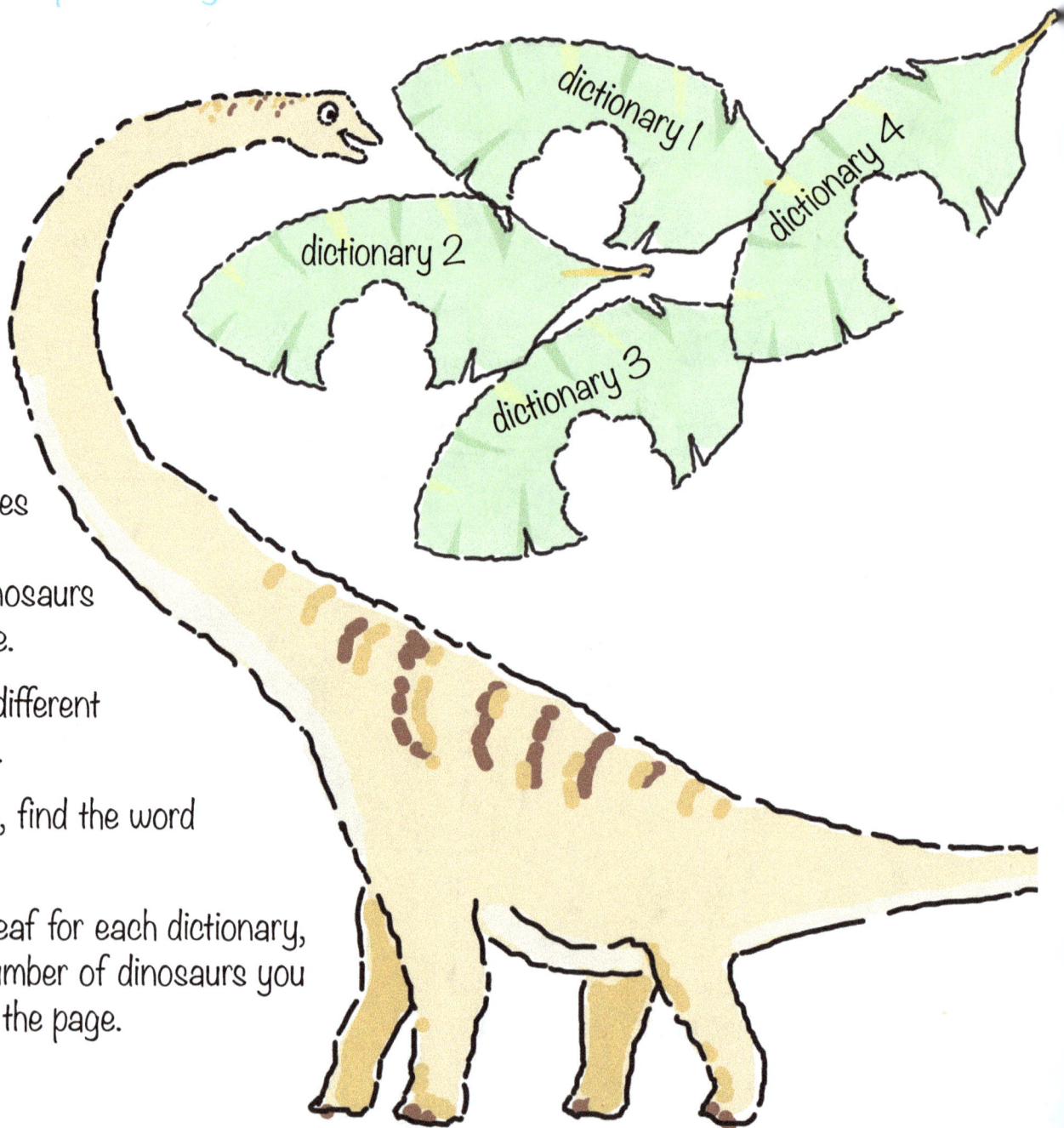

dictionary 1

dictionary 4

dictionary 2

dictionary 3

Many dictionaries show pictures of different kinds of dinosaurs on one page.

Look in 4 different dictionaries.

In each one, find the word "dinosaur."

Using one leaf for each dictionary, write the number of dinosaurs you can see on the page.

A **volcano** is a mountain or hill that sometimes explodes and pours out hot liquid rock. The Hawaiian islands were formed by volcanoes over a million years ago.

Though many volcanoes are over a million years old, a new volcano exploded out of the ocean about 50 years ago to make Earth's newest island called Surtsey Island.

Do This

- [ ] Look in 3 dictionaries to find a picture of a volcano in each one.
- [ ] Decide which one you like best.
- [ ] Show the picture to another student.
- [ ] Show the picture to your teacher.
- [ ] Draw your own volcano next to the one above.

Part 2

Putting Things in Order

Sometimes, when you have lots of things in a pile, it can be hard to find the one you need.

When you put the things in order, it's easier to see them and to find the one you want.

Order is how things are arranged.

There are many different ways to arrange things.

Here are just a few of them.

You can put them by size - from shortest to tallest. • • • • • • • • • • • • • • • •

You can put them by weight - from the **heaviest** to the lightest. • • • • • • • • • • • • •

You can put them by shades from dark to light.

You could even arrange them by the colors of the rainbow!

Do this

First you will need to gather 5 different things from around the classroom. Then you will use them to do the steps below.

- ☐ Put the 5 objects in order from shortest to tallest.

- ☐ Put the 5 things in order from the lightest to heaviest. You can choose 5 new things if you like.

- ☐ Put the things in order from darkest to lightest. You can choose 5 new things if you like.

- ☐ Find objects that are red, orange, yellow, green, blue and purple. Put the things in order of the colors of the rainbow.

- ☐ Talk about order with your teacher. Show her some different ways things can be put in order.

☐ Teacher Check

Let's Look

On this page you will do some research to find examples of order.

☐ Look around the room you are in. Try to find an area where the things seem messy and do not seem to have any kind of order. It could be a very small area or a large area. When you find one, write what you see.

_____

_____

☐ Look around the room you are in. Try to find an area where the things in it are in some kind of order. Remember, it could be a very small area or a large area. When you find one, write what you see.

_____

_____

Talk to your teacher about what kind of order you think was used.

Ask your teacher if you can do these next steps.

☐ Find an area outside the classroom where the things in it do not seem to be in order.

☐ Find an area outside the classroom where the things in it are in some kind of order.

☐ Talk to your teacher about what you found.

Let's Look

- ☐ Get a dictionary.

- ☐ Open it to the words that start with the letter A.

- ☐ Find a picture of an animal that starts with the letter A.

- ☐ When you find one, color the box with the letter A on the roll of film. • • • • •

- ☐ Now go to the pages that start with the letter B.

- ☐ Find a picture of an animal that starts with B.

- ☐ Color the box with the letter B.

- ☐ Do this for all the letters in the alphabet.

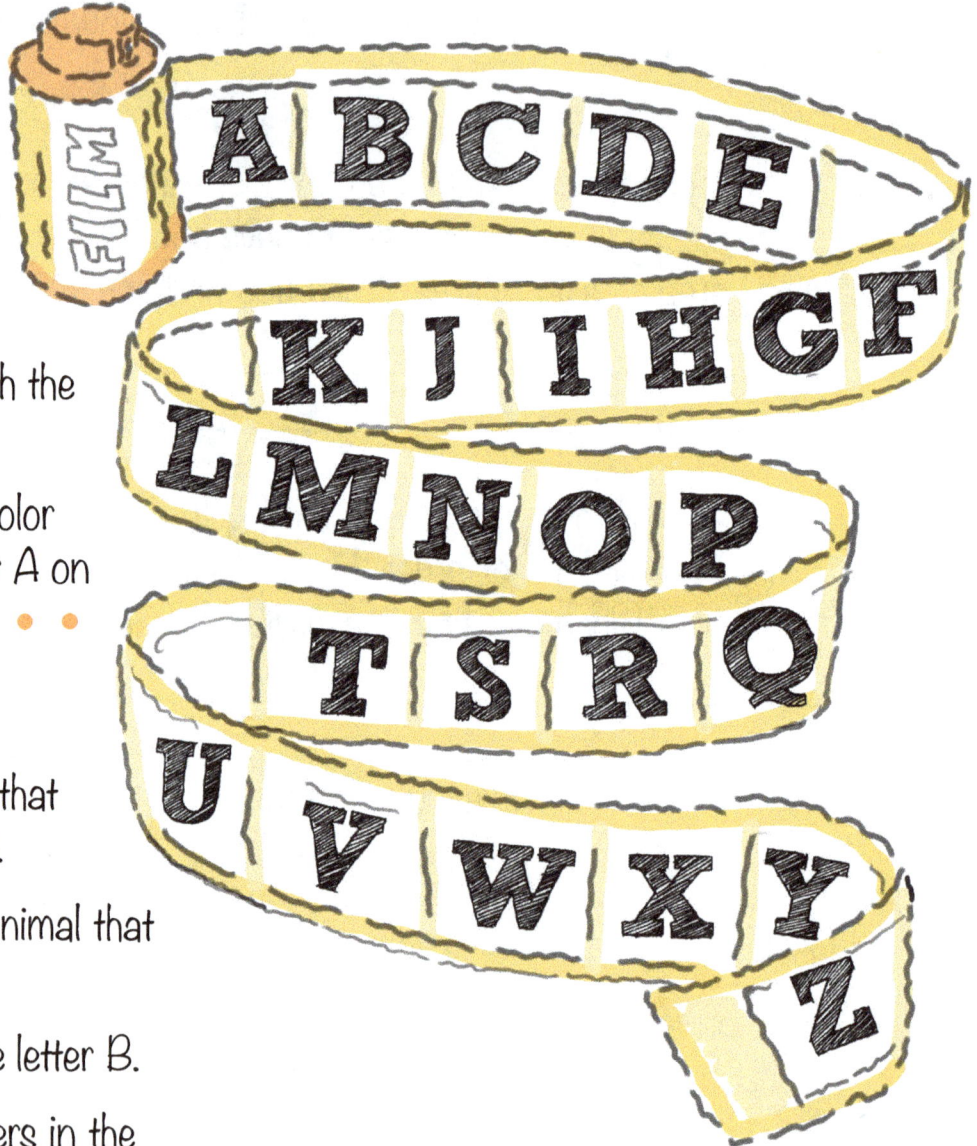

If there is a letter that does not have a picture of an animal, you can leave it blank.

FILM

A B C D E F G H I J K L M N O P Q R S T U V W X Y Z

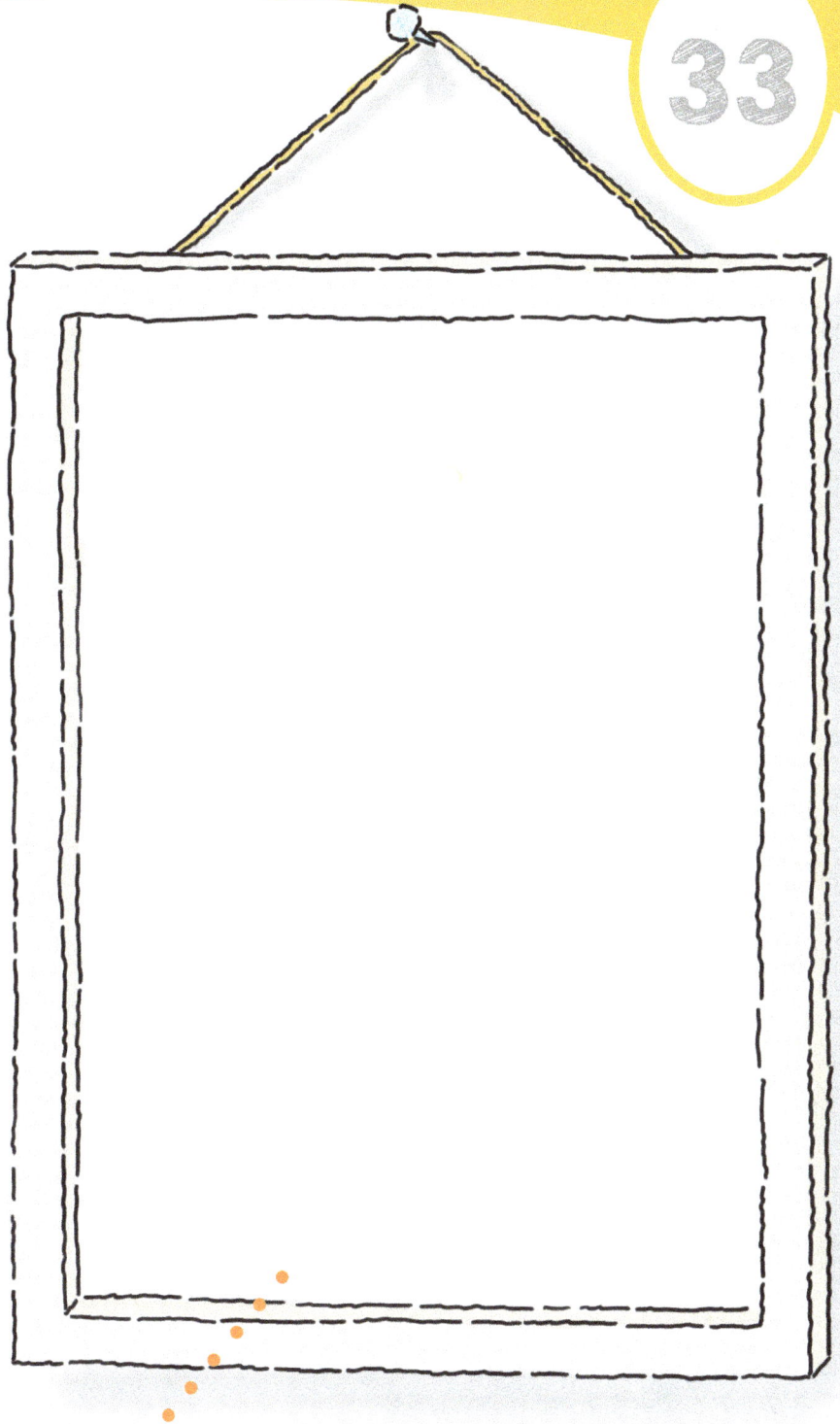

Do This

- [ ] Which picture from the last activity was your favorite?

_____

- [ ] Find the name of that animal in the dictionary.

- [ ] Read what it says.

- [ ] Copy what it says here.

_____
_____
_____
_____
_____
_____
_____
_____

- [ ] Draw that animal here. Color your picture.

- [ ] Show your drawing to another student.

Part 3

Using the Alphabet

What Are These Marks?

Δδ   Dd   Дд

Answer They are all letters. A letter is a mark that stands for a spoken sound. Every one of these marks stands for the "**d**" sound you hear in "**d**og".

Δδ   Dd   Дд
Greek   English   Russian

Before letters were invented, instead of writing words people wrote using pictures for things. Since there were thousands of things in the world, people had to learn hundreds and hundreds of marks to be able to read and write!

We are lucky to have only **26** letters to learn.

Ancient Egyptians used to write with these marks.

Do This Work with your teacher to find these countries on a map.

☐ Where you are now   ☐ Russia   ☐ Greece   ☐ Egypt

☐ **Teacher Check**

We call our letters from A to Z the **alphabet**. Our alphabet has been used by people for over 1,000 years and changed only a little bit in all that time!

I'm really glad they returned it!

The letter Z was removed from the alphabet for almost 200 years!

Fill in the letters from A to Z.

		C		
	H			
			P	
				W
Y				

- What is the **first** letter in the alphabet? _____
- What is the **last** letter in the alphabet? _____
- What letter seems nearest to the **middle**? _____
- Find the word letter in a dictionary. Read what it says.
- Now use a different dictionary to find the word letter. Read what it says.
- Talk with your teacher about whether the dictionaries gave the meaning of "letter" in exactly the same way or in a different way.

Do This

You will need a set of alphabet tiles or cards.

- [ ] 1. Arrange all the tiles face up so you can see all the letters.

- [ ] 2. Now mix the tiles around with your hands.

- [ ] 3. When the tiles are all mixed up, move the letters into order from A to Z as fast as you can.

- [ ] Do steps 1 to 3 again, only faster!

Then This

- [ ] Lay the tiles face up in a line from A to Z.

- [ ] Remove 5 tiles from the line. Turn them face down so you cannot see the letters.

- [ ] Mix them up and place them in a pile in front of you.

- [ ] Turn over one of the 5 upside-down tiles and return it to the right place in the alphabet line as fast as you can. Do this with each tile from the pile until they are all back in place.

- [ ] Do these steps again with 5 different letters.

And This

- [ ] Turn all the tiles face down and mix them around.

- [ ] As fast as you can, flip over all the tiles and line them up in order from A to Z.

- [ ] Teacher Check

ABCDEFGHIJKLMNOPQRSTUVWXYZ

Fill in the Answers

What letter comes after the letter F? ☐

What letter comes after the letter Q? ☐

What letter comes after the letter D? ☐

What letter comes before the letter B? ☐

What letter comes before the letter U? ☐

What letter comes before the letter K? ☐

What letter comes before the letter P? ☐

What letter comes before the letter C? ☐

☐ Write the letters from your answers to find out the secret message.

☐ ☐ ☐ ☐ ☐   ☐ ☐ ☐

☐ Fill in the letters that come before and after each letter shown below.

___ ⓘ ___   ___ ⓨ ___   ___ ⓝ ___

          ___ ⓡ ___   ___ ⓦ ___

ABCDEFGHIJKLMNOPQRSTUVWXYZ

Fill in the Letter

Fill in the missing letter.

__ B

V __ X

D __ F

R __ T

N __ P

L __ N

D __ F

Put the letters you wrote here to find the secret message.

☐ ☐ ☐ ☐ ☐ ☐ ☐

Fill in the Letter

Write what letter comes before or after the letter shown.

___ g

k ___

x ___

___ r

m ___

___ d

___ i

b ___

t ___

___ f

More About Order

You know the letters of the alphabet go in a certain order from A to Z.
This is called **alphabetical order**.

When words are in the same order as the alphabet they are in alphabetical order. **Alphabetical order** is useful when there are lots of words or names to keep track of.

For example
ant
bear
cat
dog
elephant

Let's Look

☐ Ask your teacher to show you examples of ways she uses alphabetical order. If you see any of the examples below, write a check mark ✓ in the box.

names of people			
names of songs			
addresses			
file folder names			
some other list of words			

☐ Ask your teacher if you can go around to ask some other adults in the school how they use alphabetical order. Put more check marks in the boxes if you see any of these. Then tell your teacher what you found out.

A **dictionary** is a book full of words and their meanings.

All the words in the dictionary are in alphabetical order.

And there is a separate section for every letter in the alphabet.

☐ Choose a dictionary you like. Going from A to Z, find the first word listed for each letter. Write the word in the box next to the letter.

A		N	
B		O	
C		P	
D		Q	
E		R	
F		S	
G		T	
H		U	
I		V	
J		W	
K		X	
L		Y	
M		Z	

☐ Show your teacher how the dictionary has different sections for different letters of the alphabet.

Letter Fun You will need a block with letters, like the one above.

- ☐ Choose a different dictionary from the one you used for the last activity.
- ☐ Roll the block, then find the beginning of the section for the letter on the top of the block.
- ☐ When you find that section put a check mark in the first box below.
- ☐ Do this 5 times. ☐ ☐ ☐ ☐ ☐

Word Fun You will need 1 letter block and 2 dictionaries to do this activity.

- ☐ Roll the letter block then write the letter in the first column below.
- ☐ Open one of the dictionaries to the first word in that section and write it in the second column.
- ☐ Open the other dictionary to the beginning of the same section. Is the word the same or different? Write your answer in the chart below.

letter rolled	first word	second dictionary same or different?

- ☐ Show your teacher 2 dictionaries that have different first words for the same section.

☐ **Teacher Check**

A B C D E F G H I J K L M N O P Q R S T U V W X Y Z

middle

beginning

end

A B C D E F G H I J K L M N O P Q R S T U V W X Y Z

You know that sections of the dictionary follow the same order as the letters in the alphabet. So words that start with a, b, c, d, e, f will be near the beginning of the dictionary.

Words that start with k, l, m, n, o will be somewhere near the middle of the dictionary.

And words that start with w, x, y, z will be near the end of the dictionary.

Do This

☐ Open the dictionary to the **middle**. What letter did you open to? _____

☐ Open the dictionary near the **beginning**. What letter did you open to? _____

☐ Open the dictionary near the **end**. What letter did you open to? _____

☐ Show your teacher what happens when you open a dictionary to a page near the beginning, the middle and the end.

ABCDEFGHIJKLMNOPQRSTUVWXYZ

Write the letters in alphabetical order.

1. _____
2. _____
3. _____
4. _____
5. _____

1. _____
2. _____
3. _____
4. _____
5. _____

1. _____
2. _____
3. _____
4. _____
5. _____

1. _____
2. _____
3. _____
4. _____
5. _____

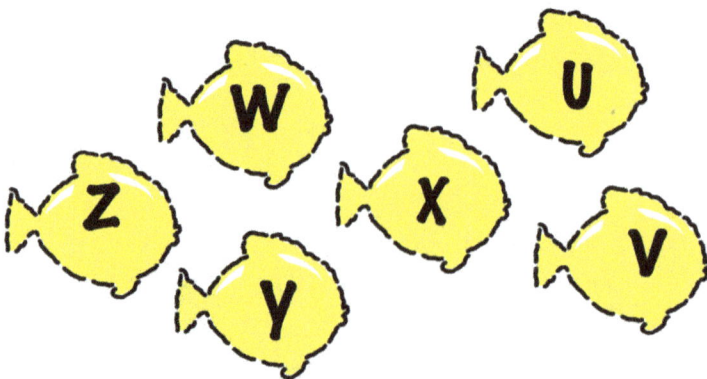

1. _____
2. _____
3. _____
4. _____
5. _____
6. _____

Putting words in alphabetical order

 car

 acorn

box

1. **a**corn

2. **b**ox

3. **c**ar

Underline the first letter in each word. Decide which word is first, which is second and so on. Then draw a line to match the word to the correct line. Last, write the words in alphabetical order.

 <u>e</u>gg

 <u>f</u>lower

 <u>d</u>og

1. _____

2. _____

3. _____

 nail

 lollipop

 mouse

1. _____

2. _____

3. _____

 hose

 igloo

 glue

1. _____

2. _____

3. _____

 quilt

 pot

 octopus

1. _____

2. _____

3. _____

49

Teacher Checke

Write these words in alphabetical order. The first one is started for you.
Remember, it can help to underline the first letter, match, then write the word.

<u>i</u>sland   1. _____

<u>k</u>ayak   2. _____

<u>j</u>ug   3. _____

<u>h</u>orse   4. _____

<u>t</u>ack   1. _____

<u>s</u>treet   2. _____

<u>v</u>iolin   3. _____

<u>u</u>mbrella   4. _____

ghost   1. _____

fish   2. _____

eagle   3. _____

house   4. _____

note   1. _____

list   2. _____

object   3. _____

man   4. _____

dance   1. _____

canoe   2. _____

engine   3. _____

apple   4. _____

bear   5. _____

velvet   1. _____

rooster   2. _____

under   3. _____

ship   4. _____

trees   5. _____

Sometimes the first letters of the words are not right next to each other in the alphabet. We can still put these words in order by knowing which letter comes before the others.

train   boat   plane

A B C D E F G H I J K L M N O P Q R S T U V W X Y Z

1.boat   2.plane   3.train

Put these words in alphabetical order.

kangaroos   foxes   bat   1._____   2._____   3._____

freeze   jump   dance   1._____   2._____   3._____

very   almost   never   1._____   2._____   3._____

fall   high   down   1._____   2._____   3._____

Use the last word in each set of answers to make a sentence below.

_____ _____   _____ _____!

Let's have some fun! You will need a partner and a set of alphabet tiles.

- [ ] Make a line with the tiles in alphabetical order from A to Z.
- [ ] Partner A closes his eyes. Partner B removes 5 tiles. Choose ones that are not right next to each other.
- [ ] Partner A opens his eyes and puts the 5 tiles in alphabetical order and writes the letters here.

☐ ☐ ☐ ☐ ☐

- [ ] Partner A puts the tiles back in the line.
- [ ] Now Partner B closes her eyes and Partner A removes 5 tiles. Choose ones that are not right next to each other.
- [ ] Partner B opens her eyes and puts the 5 tiles in alphabetical order and writes the letters here.

☐ ☐ ☐ ☐ ☐

- [ ] Partner B puts the tiles back in the line.
- [ ] Take turns playing this game until it is easy for each partner. You will need a piece of paper to draw rows of boxes like the ones above.
- [ ] Play this game with your teacher.

☐ Teacher Check

Do This

Here is another game. You will need a partner and 3 blocks with letters, like the ones above.

☐ Partner A rolls the 3 letter blocks, puts them in alphabetical order, then writes the letters in the squares under Game 1.

☐ Partner B rolls the 3 letter blocks, puts them in alphabetical order, then writes the letters in the squares under Game 2.

☐ Take turns rolling and writing.

PARTNER A

GAME 1
☐ ☐ ☐

GAME 3
☐ ☐ ☐

GAME 5
☐ ☐ ☐

GAME 7
☐ ☐ ☐

PARTNER B

GAME 2
☐ ☐ ☐

GAME 4
☐ ☐ ☐

GAME 6
☐ ☐ ☐

GAME 8
☐ ☐ ☐

A B C D E F G H I J K L M N O P Q R S T U V W X Y Z

Make a List

☐ Make a list of 5 animals you like.

☐ Now put those words in alphabetical order here.

☐ See if you can find a picture of each animal in a dictionary. Draw a star next to the ones you found a picture for.

☐ Draw the animal you like best here.

yo-yo

ball

plane

☐ Put the names of the toys in alphabetical order on the paper.

☐ See if you can find a picture of each toy in the dictionary.
☐ Draw a star next to ones you find a picture for.

☐ Write the colors of the rainbow here. See crayons on pg. 30 if you need help.

1. _____ 2. _____ 3. _____ 4. _____

5. _____ 6. _____

☐ Put the words in alphabetical order. Hint: it can be helpful to circle the first letter of each word. Then color the boxes next to each to make a different pattern.

1. _____

2. _____

3. _____

4. _____

5. _____

6. _____

Part 5

Alphabetical Order

The Second Letter of a Word

Question How do you put words in alphabetical order if they all start with the same letter?

dolphin   deer   dice   daisy

Answer Look at the second letter!

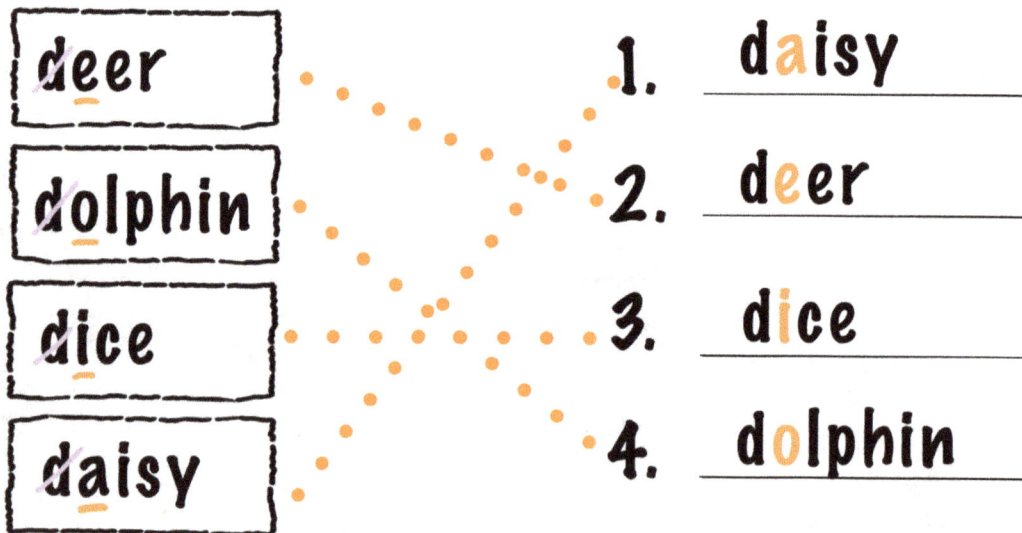

deer		1.	daisy
dolphin		2.	deer
dice		3.	dice
daisy		4.	dolphin

The first letter in the words are all the same. But the second letters are not, so we can use those to put the words in alphabetical order. Since the letter a comes before any other second letters, daisy will come first on the list.

Do This

Put these words in alphabetical order. Hint: it can be helpful to underline the second letter in the word, then match.

lobster
lamp
letter

1. _____

2. _____

3. _____

 tuba

 trumpet

 tamborine

1. _____

2. _____

3. _____

A B C D E F G H I J K L M N O P Q R S T U V W X Y Z

Put these words in alphabetical order.

cloud

cat

crown

1. _____

2. _____

3. _____

Put these words in alphabetical order by matching the word to the number then writing on the lines.

Bob

Barbara

Brian

Betsy

1. _____

2. _____

3. _____

4. _____

Here are some name tags. All the names start with the same first letter. Write the names in alphabetical order on the lines.

1. _____

2. _____

3. _____

4. _____

☐ Add these food words to the grocery list in alphabetical order.

burger

berries

bread

bananas

biscuits

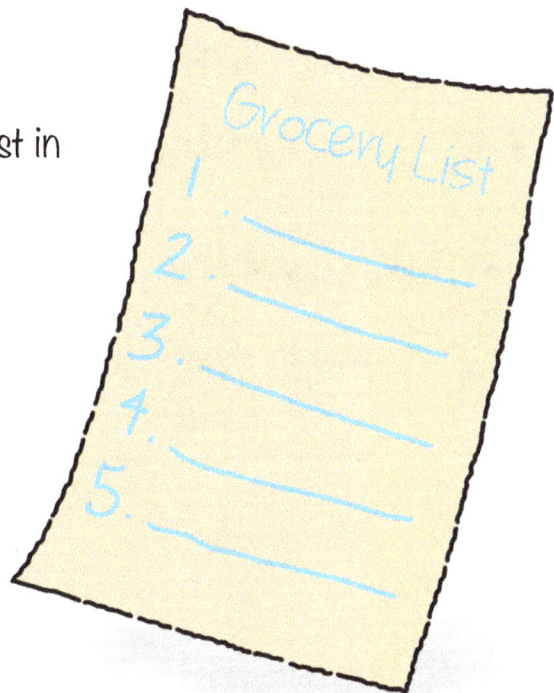

Grocery List
1. _____
2. _____
3. _____
4. _____
5. _____

A B C D E F G H I J K L M N O P Q R S T U V W X Y Z

A

Dictionary

☐ Open a dictionary to the beginning of the A words.

☐ You know that all the words in this chapter have **a** as the first letter.

☐ Find the very first **a** word. Now look at the second letter in this word. Is it **a** or **b?**

| **a** or **b** |

circle your answer

Sometimes the first word is a - meaning "one of something." If this happens look at the next word.

☐ Follow down the list of **ab** words until the second letter changes to **c.**

Write the first **ac** word here. |_____|

☐ Follow down the list of **ac** words until the second letter changes to **d.**

Write the first **ad** word here. |_____|

☐ Follow down the list of **ad** words until the second letter changes to **e.**

Write the first **ae** word here. |_____|

Keep going down the list of a words to the end of the section. Each time the second letter changes, circle that letter on the A to Z chart.

☐ **Teacher Check**

Put these words in alphabetical order.

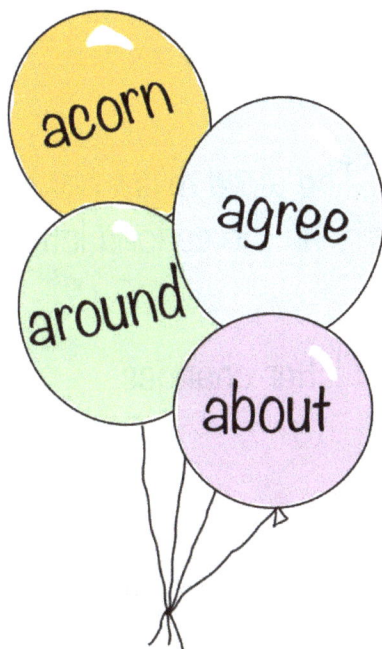

acorn

agree

around

about

1. _____

2. _____

3. _____

4. _____

☐ Now find each of these words in a dictionary as quickly as you can.

Put these words in alphabetical order.

April

arrow

always

anchor

1

2

3

4

Hint
it can be helpful to underline the second letter.

☐ Now find each of these words in a dictionary as quickly as you can.

A B C D E F G H I J K L M N O P Q R S T U V W X Y Z

B

☐ Open a dictionary to the beginning of the B words. Look at the first word. The second letter in that word will be the letter **a**.

☐ Look at the first B word in 2 other dictionaries. The word might not be the same in each dictionary but it will have the letter **a** as the second letter.

☐ Follow down the list of **ba** words until the second letter changes.

Write what the second letter changed to · · · ☐

☐ Follow down the list of **be** words until the second letter changes.

Write what the second letter changed to · · · ☐

☐ Follow down the list of **bi** words until the second letter changes.

Write what the second letter changed to · · · ☐

☐ Follow down the list of **bl** words until the second letter changes.

Write what the second letter changed to · · · ☐

Keep going down the list of b words to the end of the section. Each time the second letter changes, circle that letter on the A to Z chart.

Put these words in alphabetical order.

 bongos

 bubbles

 bag

 bear

 bin

1. _____

2. _____

3. _____

4. _____

5. _____

Hint
it can be helpful
to underline the second
letter in each word.

1. Ask 4 students to tell you a word that begins with the letter **B**. Write them here.

1. _____

2. _____

3. _____

4. _____

2. Now put those words in alphabetical order here.

1. _____

2. _____

3. _____

4. _____

ABCDEFGHIJKLMNOPQRSTUVWXYZ

Write these words in alphabetical order. Hint - it can help to underline the second letter of each word. The first one is done for you.

crane   1. cat _____

cat   2. cellar _____

cellar   3. crane _____

cute   4. cute _____

food   1. _____

fast   2. _____

fun   3. _____

flash   4. _____

doze   1. _____

dance   2. _____

deep   3. _____

dim   4. _____

horse   1. _____

hands   2. _____

hurry   3. _____

help   4. _____

eel   1. _____

energy   2. _____

eagle   3. _____

elephant   4. _____

inside   1. _____

island   2. _____

igloo   3. _____

imagine   4. _____

☐ Teacher Check

ABCDEFGHIJKLMNOPQRSTUVWXYZ

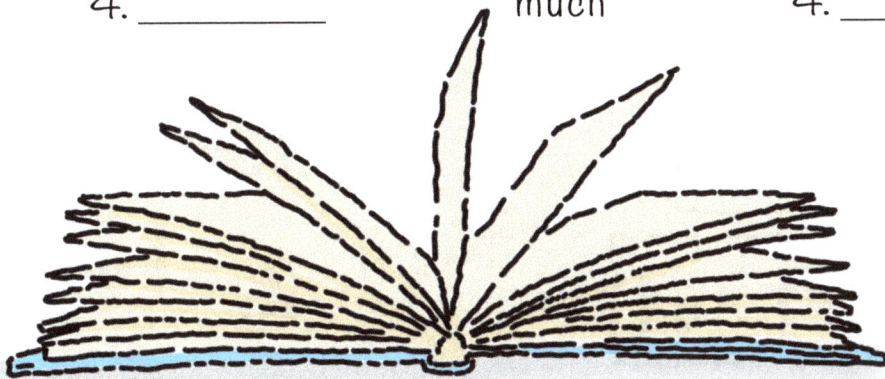

Write these words in alphabetical order. Hint - it can help to underline the second letter of each word.

whale   1. _____   move   1. _____

will   2. _____   miss   2. _____

world   3. _____   many   3. _____

went   4. _____   much   4. _____

Write these words in alphabetical order.

tree   1. _____ ☐

telephone   2. _____ ☐   Choose a dictionary. Look for these words. Put a check mark in the box each time you find one.

talk   3. _____ ☐

time   4. _____ ☐

Question How do you put words in alphabetical order when they start with the same first and second letter?

internet

ink

inch

insect

Answer Maybe you guessed - look at the third letter!

ink

internet

inch

insect

1. inch

2. ink

3. insect

4. internet

A B C D E F G H I J **K** L M N O P Q **R** S T U V W X Y Z

The first two letters in the words above are the same. The third letters are c, k, s and t. Since the letter c comes earlier in the alphabet than the other letters, the word inch comes first on the list.

Write these words in alphabetical order.

path   1. _____   rent   1. _____

paper   2. _____   reward   2. _____

park   3. _____   rest   3. _____

panda   4. _____   rectangle   4. _____

Write these words in alphabetical order.

strap   1. _____   ☐

still   2. _____   ☐   Choose a dictionary.
                                     Look for these
stay   3. _____   ☐   words. Put a check
                                     mark in the box
stem   4. _____   ☐   each time you find
                                     one.

Write these words in alphabetical order. Hint - it can help to underline the third letter of each word. The first one is done for you.

slow   1. slab

slab   2. slime

slug   3. slow

slime   4. slug

yet   1. _____

yell   2. _____

yesterday   3. _____

year   4. _____

gate   1. _____

gave   2. _____

game   3. _____

gap   4. _____

lump   1. _____

lunch   2. _____

lucky   3. _____

lullaby   4. _____

drill   1. _____

dress   2. _____

droop   3. _____

drum   4. _____

move   1. _____

Monday   2. _____

mother   3. _____

moon   4. _____

Choose a dictionary you like. Find the word dictionary in it.

Write the word that comes **before** the word dictionary and the word that comes **after**.

before   **di**□ _____

dictionary _____

after   **di**□ _____

□ Think of a word. Write it here. _____

□ Find your word in the dictionary.

□ Write the word that comes **before** your word and the word that comes **after**.

before   _____

your word   _____

after   _____

A B C D E F G H I J K L M N O P Q R S T U V W X Y Z

☐ Choose a dictionary you like. Find the words below. Write the word that comes before and the word that comes after.

☐ Put the third letter of each word in the box.

pi☐ _____

pie _____

pi☐ _____

aw☐ _____

away _____

aw☐ _____

do☐ _____

dolphin _____

do☐ _____

Question   What do you do if the word begins with the same first, second and third letter?

sank   sand   sang

Answer   You probably guessed - look at the fourth letter!

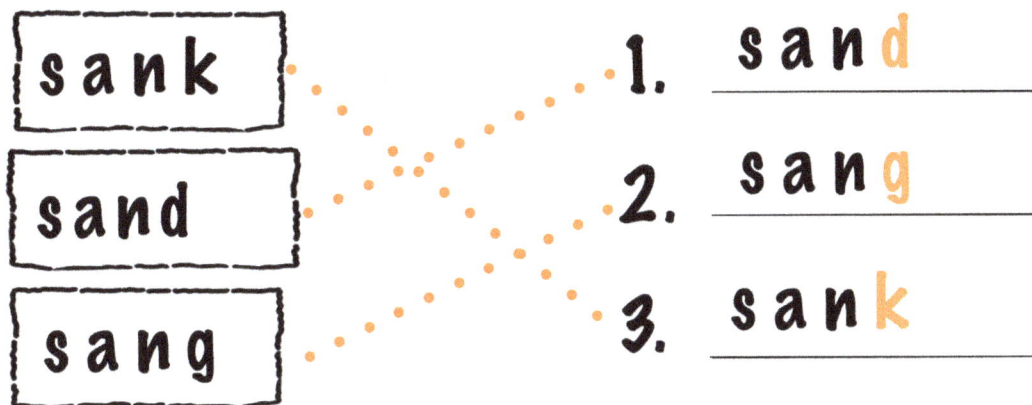

sank
sand
sang

1. **s a n d**
2. **s a n g**
3. **s a n k**

A B C **D** E F **G** H I J **K** L M N O P Q R S T U V W X Y Z

Put these words in alphabetical order

street	1._____	black	1._____	craft	1._____
strong	2._____	blank	2._____	crack	2._____
straight	3._____	blade	3._____	crab	3._____

Part 6

A Few More Things

You already know that a dictionary is a book full of words and their meanings.

You know that there is a section for every letter in the alphabet.

And you know that the words in the sections are in alphabetical order.

Each word listed in the dictionary is called an entry word. To make it easier to see the entry words, they are usually printed larger and darker or even in a different color than the rest of the words on the page.

entry word

chair 1. a piece of furniture that you sit on, with a seat, legs and a back.

meaning of the word

entry word

chair 1. a seat with a back for one person.

It is important to know that different dictionaries may explain the meaning of the same word in different ways.

A B C D E F G H I J K L M N O P Q R S T U V W X Y Z

Find the word **chair** in 2 different dictionaries.

How does the entry word look in each one? Do they look the same, or different? Mark your answer.

◯ same   ◯ different

Find the word **kangaroo** in 3 different dictionaries.

How does the entry word look in each one? Do they look the same or different? Mark your answer.

◯ same   ◯ different

Read the meaning of kangaroo in each dictionary. Are the meanings written the same way or are they different? Mark your answer.

◯ same   ◯ different

Show your teacher an example of how different dictionaries sometimes explain the meaning of a word in different ways.

A **guide** is a person or thing that helps to show the way.

Since there are so many words that begin with the same letter and so many pages, most dictionaries put a word or two at the top corner of every page to help you find words more easily. In other words, to **guide** you through the dictionary.

These are called **guide words**. They are there to help show which part of the dictionary you are in and what words are on that page.

guide words

These guide words mean the first word on the page is **fit** and the last word on the page is **float**.

fit ▸ float

fit
five
fix
float

flock ▸ food

flock
flood
floor
food

guide words

These guide words mean the first word on the page is **flock** and the last word on the page is **food**.

You can use guide words on a page to tell if you are getting close to the word you are looking for.

Let's Look

Find the word **shark** in a dictionary. Look at the guide words at the top.

Write the guide words here. _____ and _____

Write the **first** and **last** word on the page here. _____ and _____

Let's try using some guide words to help us find words in a dictionary!

Choose a dictionary. Find the word pipe.

Write the guide words that are at the top of the page.

_____ and _____

Write the first and last words on the page here.

_____ and _____
first   last

Choose a different dictionary. Find the word pipe.

Write the guide words that are at the top of the page.

_____ and _____

Write the first and last words on the page here.

_____ and _____
first   last

Are the guide words in the second dictionary the **same** or **different** than the first dictionary?

Write your answer _____

Choose a dictionary you like. Find the word monkey.

Write the guide words that are at the top of the page.

_____ and _____

Was there a picture of a monkey in this dictionary?

Yes ◯   No ◯

Find the word queen.

Write the guide words that are at the top of the page.

_____ and _____

Was there a picture of a queen in this dictionary?

Yes ◯   No ◯

Find the word elephant.

Write the guide words that are at the top of the page.

_____ and _____

Was there a picture of an elephant in this dictionary?

Yes ◯   No ◯

☐ Teacher Check

ABCDEFGHIJKLMNOPQRSTUVWXYZ

Choose your own word. Write it here. _____

Find this word in a dictionary. Write the guide words that are at the top of the page.
_____ and _____

Was there a picture to go with your word?

Yes ◯   No ◯

Ask another student to choose a word. Write it here. _____

Find this word in a dictionary. Write the guide words that are at the top of the page.
_____ and _____

Was there a picture to go with this word?

Yes ◯   No ◯

Ask another student to choose a word. Write it here. _____

Find this word in a dictionary. Write the guide words that are at the top of the page.
_____ and _____

Was there a picture to go with this word?

Yes ◯   No ◯

Teacher Check ☐

This workbook has told you many things about the dictionary.

Here are some things you may have learned.

- A dictionary is a book that gives the meanings of words.

- Dictionaries have a section for each letter in the alphabet.

- Different dictionaries have different pictures.

- Dictionaries put words in alphabetical order.

- Words can be put in alphabetical order by the first letter in the word.

- When words have the same first letter, they can be put in alphabetical order by the second or third letter, and so on.

- Not all dictionaries explain the meaning of a word the same way.

- Entry words are usually **larger** and **darker** than the other words and are sometimes a different color.

- Guide words help show what part of the dictionary you are in and what words are on the page.

Tell your teacher some of the things you liked best in this workbook.

AWESOME!

_____

has
finished

Using the Dictionary

Workbook 1

_____
Date

_____
Student

_____
Teacher